Water the Mud

Water the Mud

poems by

Joel E. Jacobson

This chapbook is

A Poetic Matter

Arvada, Colorado

for my boys

CONTENTS

FANTINE

When Fantine falls
into the snow, incapable
of making herself
worthy of even the poorest
men, we pity her,
beg her not to sell
her teeth; then
we practically
kiss the feet
of Val Jean
when he swoops in
and snatches her
from the claws
of Javert.

When the harlot
falls before Jesus,
wipes away
the city muck
with her face,
we've already
judged and shut
her out—
and we already know
(if we've been
reading along)
that Jesus
will forgive her.

What we don't know,
sitting at the dinner table
in awkward, interrupted
silence, is the aroma
of forgiveness, wafting
about her empty,
alabaster jar.

SMASHED GRAPES

That light rising
on the horizon,
the light that within weeks
fades hats, shirts, and
everything else you use
to protect against the sun,
that light is the sound of
those you never have time for.

∞

Work is inevitable.
The inspired and the sloth
must punch the clock
on the docks fishing
in the vineyards picking
or simply sticking around
the town square waiting
for work to fall
like crumbs from a table.

∞

The loudest grumbles come
from the men who worked
a full day, proudest
of having picked the most
and the best, convinced
that they deserve

more than the bums
who came in
at the last minute,
and, as if worthy,
gleaned a poem
from smashed grapes
and the waning minutes
of day.

JAR FULL OF GOLD

The old man spent his life
saving nuggets for the jar.
Before he went to sleep
every night, he counted
what he earned that day
and listened to the rich melody
of his exponential wealth
clanking into the clay jar.
He remembered how he came
by every ounce of gold
(either by not spending
or spending significantly
less than he should have)
and chose one coin every night
to hold in his sleep like a child
holds his favorite stuffed animal,
though the old man never outgrew
his gold. The man died
in his sleep, grasping one
tarnished coin as if he was
trying to smuggle
a little contraband from now
into the land of tomorrow.
It was his favorite because
he didn't have to spend it
on that one family
vacation when they all
had water and rice
for every meal.

No wonder he showed up
on the steps of eternity
missing both a hand and a heart.

His children, meanwhile,
massaged the rigor mortis
and the coin from the corpse's
hand. The rope was tied
and the jar already hoisted
when they tossed the last
coin in with the others,
as if wishing at a well.
Accounts settled, they made
the servant apply the blindfolds
and supply the sticks
(broom handles, actually)
and spin them dizzy
(to the other side of the room)
so they could whack
at the gold their father
never let them touch.
While they played piñata
with themselves in the corner,
the servant took down the jar
and walked into the night,
a soft, syncopated jingle.

One boy thumped something
blindly, harder when he heard

the screams. In the morning
the servant returned empty handed.
He sifted through the pile
of unconscious bodies.
The boy on bottom,
the dead one,
had removed his blindfold.
The rest left theirs in place,
content with the feel
of crunching glass
and gold raining
from the ceiling.

KNOWING

A boy walks down to the lake,
leaving the others, the talkers,
back in the echoing camp chapel.
Making his way to the far side
where the embankment rises
several feet, he sits down,
fingers a small, rough rock,
comes to know its sharp edges
and flicks it, counting the skips.

A man died this morning.
Not his own dad, not the strong, gentle giant,
but a weak, sick man, a shadow
who refused to acknowledge
that he was dying, dead.
The dead man's son was there
in the chapel when he got word
and drove home without really saying
goodbye to anybody. The rest of them
sang songs and took communion,
trying to understand God
on the morning a father died.

Another rock. Fourfivesix—
A small trout flips from the water,
nips a bug, and dives back into
the shallow little lake.

There are only two types of fathers:
living and dead. Sure, there's the drunkard,
the absent, the violent, the fill in the blank
but those men offer a hollow existence
in the lives of their children, dead
without ever dying.
 And the good ones?
It's the good ones who actually die first.

The dining hall bell rattles birds from the trees,
sharpness from morning's chill.
Hearing the girls squawk—
small wonder the fish ever leapt at all—
the boy climbs to his feet, dirt smudging
his jeans, his canvas shoes.
A small trail of pebbles plop
into the water. The boy
takes his time walking back,

knowing a little more
of what he doesn't understand.

BECOMING ART

for T.W.

A painting can't picture itself.
An idea isn't realized
without first being birthed
through the prism of the artist.

In time, thick, grieving strokes blot out
the idea of self (pencil-outlined as a child)
and the subsequent color palette,
however sad or beautiful,
is no longer sensible or appealing.

What it takes to just sit there
and feel each wet brush-stroke
each blackening shadow
until the painting has depth
and dries.

Tokens used to inspire eventually expire,
end up on sale for 25 cents in the back corner
of a tired thrift store. It's difficult to decipher
which is uglier,

                              the dust or the paint.

The parable of the ten virgins couldn't happen today because cell phones run on batteries. We've heard the stories of those who forgot their phone charger but still stayed up late texting and facebooking, ~~checking~~ defining their status, and others'. I'll shop 'til my phone drops and drop myself into a dead sleep, salvation. If a tree falls in the forest and nobody tweets about it, does the tree matter? Because they are not here in front of me, there are no tornadoes or tsunamis or economic crises; there is no knock on the door, no parents demanding I wake up, nobody sweeping me off my feet or out of my bed, and there surely isn't a bzzzzz bzzzzz telling me I must read the most epic apocalyptic text ever because my phone died. Plus, I'm not a virgin.

What Comes Of It—

"I have seen the moment of my greatness flicker,
And I have seen the eternal footman hold my coat, and snicker
And in short, I was afraid."
        from T.S. Eliot's "The Love Song of J. Alfred Prufrock"

1.
Because 90 percent of me is drowning.
Because the remaining ten percent bobs and gasps.
Because all of me worries—
like coarse sandpaper on a wood block
like zebra mussels anchored on a wood dock
like sour salt on a raw tongue—
when all I have to do is float in the current
like a lobster in warming waters
or simply stand up and get out.
I am still what I fear.

2.
Over a hundred years, an oak tree
develops roots like a subway system
intertwined beneath city foundations.
Watered with change and pre-paid passes
civilization sprouts, scrapes into the sky,
etches away the blue hues
and peels up fields like a construction worker
opening an orange for lunch.
No oak can withstand the steel
stampede, the urban sprawl,

so it gets chopped from the top
down—an umbrella stripped to spire.
Chain the base. With the fire-power
of a big rig, rip it out. Don't worry
about the tree-houses or tire swings—
children need to grow up anyways.

Cut it down.

Then, is it still a tree?

3.
Model Airplanes: caged in plastic molds
even a young child can hold
and crack apart, just to paste the halves
back together, differently. The gobbed glue
and wrinkled decals beg for empathy
or pride and the entire thing is either a good
first try or a failure. Whether it falls apart
or not (it happens over time: the paint chips,
the missiles fall off and sometimes a wing),
what comes of it—a dream or a man?

4.
These pieces fit like painted
manikins and man-he-cants
filling wombs and elastic tombs
and entire tubes of sand-seconds
in between the bulbs of earth's

hourglass. Maybe I can still muster fistfuls
of splintered hope, thread each one
into each sun, waiting for every
worry to become shallow and undone.

Mosaic

I am a wine glass,
melted down
gently blown
and etched
into a limited
edition of one.
Fill me
with the most
expensive wine
and throw me
against the wall.
Break me into
pricey dust
because I can't
see God anyways.

I am a wall,
framed
insulated
dry-walled
textured
to look new,
pleasing
to the eye
complementary
to the art
hanging from
drilled holes
and plastic

anchors.
Sink
a sledge
hammer
in the middle
of my chest.
Tear down
my facade,
bare my bones.
Help me undo
the builder's
mistake.

When God seems
to have moved on
without me,
a mosaic
of dust and shards
and nails soaked
in wine, your cupped
hands bear me,
holding tightly
until I can stand,
until your hands
are full of holes.

In Stopping

"When a woman has a discharge of blood
for many days . . . that continues beyond
her period, she will be unclean as long as
she has the discharge."
    Leviticus 15:25 (NIV)

In stopping to ask,
"Who touched me?"
a woman is healed,
and a girl dies—
yet both had faith.
I would easily
rush to the street
and beg for Jesus
to heal my dying child;
I would slice
through the crowd
just to brush up
against his cloak
and be okay
getting struck
by lightning
because either way
the bleeding stops.

But my prayers
would have ceased
years and years ago,
died with the hearts of men

who made sure to mention
all that was unclean,
all that was me.

In the face of laughter
Jesus mends the dead
and bleeding,
though I've only seen
the faithful, determined
to experience a miracle,
be embalmed
and buried
with the rest.

Me of little faith,
stuck in the middle
of the story,
the middle of the crowd
pressing in
on a busy Jesus.

WATER THE MUD

I once wanted to grow
an apple, so I buried one whole—
stem, hypantheum, ovule, and all.
A squirrel dug it up, chattered
over it until a snake bit and killed
it. A crow carried the snake away
and my apple rotted in the afternoon sun.

I once wanted to write a sestina,
so I picked my six words,
wrangled them with barbed wire
to the pattern they belonged to—
trust me, I knew where the words went
and the idea was definitive
like the end of the rainbow—
and waited for the poem to sprout.

I told a friend about Jesus once,
I could see so clearly how he
could be saved from so much calamity
and his story became words to me—
his life like an apple.

Ideas—language—hearts
need water to grow
beyond the mud.
If mud is all we see,
they become laundry
drowning on the washboard.

At the Well

A puddle of water
looks like a muddy mess
until the breeze feathers
the surface
and, like a light touch
on a water glass,
leaves a .

Speaking in metaphors,
bringing to light her secret
story of man after man after—

We too
often don't know
the voice of God
until he has
passed us by, us
hiding in the dry
well of our own selves:

Eventually he says,
"I am he" but mostly
we see smudged prints
on the glasses
stacked in the sink
waiting to be washed.

There will always dirt;
there will always be water.
Look up and see the fields,
the thirsty hearts.

NOTES

Original versions of these poems appeared as a collaboration with fellow teacher and artist Nicole Brown. We set out to respond to the words and stories of Jesus found in the Gospels as presented in a series of sermons titled *Storytellers*. To access the audio of those talks, please visit www.grace-alone.org. The scripture references for each poem are listed below.

"Fantine": Luke 7:36-50

"Smashed Grapes": Matthew 20:1-19

"Jar Full of Gold": Luke 16:1-15

"Knowing": Luke 13:11-31

"Becoming Art": Matthew 11:25-30

"Oil For the Lamp": Matthew 25:1-13

"What Comes of it": Luke 12:22-34

"Mosaic": Luke 7:1-9

"In Stopping": Luke 8:40-56

"At the Well": John 4:1-42

www.ingramcontent.com/pod-product-compliance
Lightning Source LLC
Chambersburg PA
CBHW031531040426
42445CB00009B/492